Most Popular Jungle Animals

Billy Grinslott & Kinsey Marie Books

ISBN - 9781965098301

The Harpy Eagle is considered one of the largest and most powerful raptors globally. The length of their rear talons is about 4 to 5 inches long, the same as a grizzly bear's claws. Their talons give them enough power and grip to lift and hold prey while they are flying. They can fly 50 miles per hour. Harpies build massive nests, about ten feet wide. One nest contains more than 300 branches.

Toucans are very colorful birds with a long beak, that they use to pick fruit out of the trees. When toucans sleep, they turn their head so that their long bill rests on their back and their tail is folded over their head. The toucan's beak appears quite heavy but is actually light.

The Flame Bowerbird got its name, because its rich orange colors blend into yellow, making it look like it has flames on its body. It is one of the most eye-catching birds. Bowerbirds like to decorate their nest with attention getting items or shiny objects.

Scarlet Macaws are the largest type of parrot. Macaws can live for a long time. They are beautiful, smart, and can even mimic human speech. It uses its massive, hooked beak as a third foot to grasp trees for climbing. They make great pets.

Cassowaries are big birds. They can grow to six feet tall. They have a crown on their head. They also have large feet with very sharp claws. They have strong legs and can run 31 miles per hour and jump 7 ft straight in the air. One last cool fun fact is they lay green eggs.

Hornbills have a long curved yellow bill. The most notable feature is it has a beautiful casque or horn present on top of its large yellow bill. The color of the casque or horn is yellow for females and reddish to yellow for males.

Red junglefowl look and act like farm roosters. They are very noisy, vocal birds and call mostly in the morning, just like roosters. The tail of the male Red junglefowl can grow up to 11 inches and contains 14 feathers. Red junglefowl are social and typically live in flocks. They have vibrant colors.

Water Monitors are the Komodo Dragon's cousin. They are a type of large lizard. They are very intelligent and have a great sense of smell. They use their tail as weapons by swatting things. They are good swimmers. They eat almost anything they come across. They are very fast despite their massive size. They can also climb trees.

The anaconda is another popular snake. Anacondas are the world's largest snake. It can grow up to 30 feet long, about as long as your school bus. A full-grown anaconda can weigh up to 550 pounds. Anacondas are constrictors. They kill their prey by squeezing it to death just like a boa constrictor.

Boa Constrictors are non-venomous Snakes. They get their name because they wrap themselves around things. They have a lot of strength when they wrap around something, they can crush it. It's best not to let a boa constrictor wrap around you, because they can be hard to get off and can hurt you.

Green Tree Boa. Their color at birth is red, orange or yellow, which changes to bright green within their first year. They live in jungles and can be found slithering and hanging from the trees. Their green color acts as camouflage to help hide them in the leaves. They are more active at night. They have bright yellow eyes.

Pythons are one of the largest snakes. Unlike other snakes, they are non-venomous. Instead, they have four rows of back teeth in their upper jaw and two rows of teeth in their lower jaw that they use for grabbing prey. Then they wrap their body around it and squeeze it, to suffocate it before swallowing it.

Crocodiles are the most dangerous reptiles in the world. They have very few natural enemies. Crocodiles have the strongest bite of any other animal. Their bite force is estimated to be several thousand pounds per square inch. They can regrow new teeth. They have a specialized groove in their jaws that allows new teeth to grow to replace the ones they lose. Over their lifetime, they can grow and replace thousands of teeth. They have sensory organs on their snout, that allows them to pick up the slightest vibration in the water. allowing the crocodile to detect even the smallest disturbances made by potential prey or threats.

Despite their large size and clumsy appearance on land, crocodiles are excellent swimmers. They use their powerful tails to propel themselves through the water and can reach speeds, exceeding 20 miles per hour. Crocodiles primarily consume fish, but they also prey on mammals, birds, and other reptiles. They are known for their death roll technique, where they spin their bodies to tear apart prey or dismember larger animals. Crocodiles have been on the earth for a very long time, longer than most other animals.

Capybaras are a rodent. Their closest relatives are guinea pigs. They are great swimmers. Capybaras can dive and stay underwater for up to 5 minutes at a time, often falling asleep in the water while keeping their nose on the edge of the bank. They are also very agile on land. Capybara prefer to live in large herds of around 10-20 and are seen hanging out with other animals. They are vegetarians and eat aquatic plants, grasses, barks and sugar cane.

Pangolin means roller. When a Pangolin is in danger, it will roll up into a ball and can be rolled around. They have a hard shell that also protects them. There are eight species of pangolin, and they are built like an armadillo. They have long sharp front claws they use for digging up food, like insects and worms.

The Tapir is one of the strangest looking animals on the planet. Their long snout is prehensile, meaning it's made to wrap around and grab things. Tapirs use their noses to grab fruit, leaves, and other food. An adult tapir can eat as much as 75 pounds of food in a single day. Tapirs are among the most primitive mammals on Earth, changing very little over the past 20 million years. Their closest living relatives, therefore, are horses, rhinoceroses, and zebras.

The spotted-tailed quoll, or tiger quoll, is about the size of a domestic cat but with shorter legs and a pointed face. There are four species of quolls. The Tiger quoll has a sturdy build and powerful sharp teeth. It has the second most powerful bite relative to the body size of any living carnivore. Quolls are nocturnal, spending the days in their dens and coming out at night to forage for food. Their young are born the size of a grain of rice, that's really small.

The sloth gets its name because it moves really slow. Sloths move so slowly that algae and fungi have time to land and grow on them. Sloths are blind. They are faster in water than on land. It takes sloths 30 days to digest their food because their metabolism is so slow. They are 3 times stronger than humans.

Sloth Bears live in tropical areas and jungles. Less than 20,000 sloth bears remain in the wild. The sloth bear got its name for its long, thick claws and unusual teeth. Sloth bears are the only bears to routinely carry their young on their backs. Sloth bears have shaggy, dusty-black coats; pale, short-haired muzzles; and long, curved claws which they use to dig up termites and ants.

The sun bear is a species of bear that is native to the tropical forest regions and jungles. Sun bears are named for the golden patches of fur on their chests, which some people say resemble a rising sun. They are related to the Asian black bear.

Dholes are called the whistling dog. Dholes produce unusual whistling calls to identify each other when the pack is scattered, allowing them to reassemble the pack. Dholes live in packs of 5-12 individuals. A pack of dholes will have a main pair of dogs that are the packs leaders. Dholes are not known for their speed, but they can reach 45 mph and jump vertically up to seven feet. They live in dens, built underground.

Howler monkeys are called that because of the loud noises they make. Howlers make up the highest percentage of the primates in the areas that they occupy. Howler monkeys are one of the few primate species with different coat colors in males and females. Males have a black coat, while females are blonde. They live in tall rainforest trees in groups of between 4 and 19 members. They travel from tree to tree in search of food, walking from limb to limb, rather than jumping.

There are both monkeys and Chimpanzees in Africa. They are skilled climbers and like hanging out in trees. There are 200 species of monkeys and chimps. They are smart and even use rocks and sticks as tools. The howler monkey makes the loudest noises. Monkeys and chimpanzees love to eat fruits and vegetables, like bananas. Grooming each other is a sign of affection and helps build strong relationships.

Bonobos and chimpanzees look similar and share 98% of their DNA with humans. Making them our closest living relatives. Bonobo groups are more peaceful and are led by females, rather than males like most other monkeys. Bonobos are highly playful. They love to wrestle and chase each other. They also laugh and giggle when tickled.

Panamanian night monkey, as its name implies, this monkey is nocturnal and most active at night. Because they have a round face and big eyes, they are often referred to as an owl monkey. Their eyes are made to see at night, but they can't see colors like humans do. They are the world's only truly nocturnal monkey. The Panamanian night monkey is a small monkey, with males weighing 2 pounds and females weighing less than 2 pounds.

Orangutans are the biggest and heaviest tree-dwelling animal. They've got long arms. They eat with their feet. They build nests to sleep in. Some orangutans use sticks and rocks as tools.

Gorillas have hands and feet like humans including thumbs and big toes. Some gorillas have learned to use sign language to communicate with humans. Gorillas pound their chest as a type of communication. People share around 98% of our DNA with gorillas. They are one of the biggest, most powerful living primates. They have 16 different types of calls. Gorillas live in small groups called troops or bands. They live up to 35 years.

Okapis belong to the Giraffe family. But are related to the zebra. That's why they have partial zebra stripes. They can stand on their back feet to eat leaves off trees. That's how they got the nickname of TreeHugger. Wild Okapis only live in the regions of Congo jungle in Africa.

Bongos are the largest of the forest antelopes. Native people believe if they eat or touch a bongo, they will have spasms like epileptic seizures. Because of this weird superstition, bongos have been relatively unharmed in their native ranges. Bongos are great jumpers but prefer to go under or around obstacles. Both males and females have spiraled shaped horns. They are easily identified due to their vertical side stripes. They can grow some very impressive horns, unlike deer that grow and shed their antlers every year, the bongo keeps theirs throughout their lives.

Gaurs give out roaring calls, which can last for hours. It is very difficult for humans to approach Gaurs because they are extremely shy and cautious animals. In 2001, a gaur became the first cloned animal among endangered species. Their horns are tilted backwards and have a inward curvature. The Gaur is a social animal. They generally live in group size of about 30 to 40 animals. The Gaur, also known as the Indian Bison, is the largest species of wild cattle.

Jaguars are the third largest cat in the world. Known for its jump, the word jaguar means, he who kills with one leap. They can run at speeds of up to 50 mph over short distances. They are the second fastest big cat in the world. Jaguars have the strongest bite of all cats. They also roar like other big cats. They also like to swim. Jaguars are active during both day and night. Jaguars live primarily in the rainforest.

Leopards are sometimes confused with cheetahs because of their markings. The cheetah has black spots. The leopard has round markings called rosettes. Leopards are some of the strongest cats on earth. They can climb trees even while carrying another animal. They are very elusive and good at hiding. They can run up to 35 miles per hour. They can jump 20 feet in one bounce and jump 10 feet high. That's amazing.

Male lions are known as the king of the jungle because of their raw power and strength. Lions don't fear other animals. The roar of a male lion can be heard 5 miles away. Lions like to live in groups known as a pride. Male lions have mains and females do not. Female lions gather most of the food and male lions protect the herd and the young cubs, baby lions.

Tigers are considered one of the most beautiful cats by many, because of their astonishing looks and black stripes. Tigers are the largest amongst all the wild cats. They are strong and can knock things down with one swipe of their paw. Tiger cubs are born blind until their eyes develop. Tigers live for 25 years, and they love to swim and play in the water.

Look there's a hippopotamus, also called a hippo. They are the second largest land animal. They have the largest mouth of any land animal. To stay cool, they spend most of their time in the water. Hippos can hold their breath for up to five minutes underwater. When submerged, their ears and nostrils fold shut to keep water out. They sweat an oily red liquid which helps protect their skin and acts as a sunblock, too! Cool, huh?

There's a rhinoceros, also called a rhino. They are huge and can run as fast as a car, up to 55 miles per hour. They have a long horn on their nose that is made from the same stuff as our fingernails. Rhinos have very poor eyesight. They communicate through honks and sneezes. They snort to warn other animals when they get to close. They love playing in the mud and water to keep cool and keep insects from biting them.

Elephants are the largest land animal. They have huge ears. They can grab stuff with their trunks. Elephants eat all day long. They can't jump like other animals and humans. Elephants communicate with vibrations in the ground. Baby elephants can stand within 20 minutes after birth. Elephants are very smart, they never forget anything. Elephants purr like cats do.

Author Page

Billy Grinslott & Kinsey Marie Books

ISBN - 9781965098301

www.ingramcontent.com/pod-product-compliance
Lightning Source LLC
Chambersburg PA
CBHW060833270326
41933CB00002B/70